# FIGHTERS

Michael Heatley

**Exeter Books**

**NEW YORK**

A Bison Book

Page 1: *A pilot's-eye view of the General Dynamics F-16 reveals the expected complex array of dials – but no conventional control column. The F-16's 'side stick' controller on the right of the picture is linked to a 'fly-by-wire' system that replaces the usual mechanical linkages between cockpit and controls, while a head-up display projects vital information into the pilot's line of vision to make this a true warplane of the future.*

Page 2: *Two Panavia Tornados from the Royal Air Force's No 9 Squadron on operations. The variable geometry Mach 2 Tornado was the product of a three-country consortium formed by Germany, Britain and Italy, and has proved a potent addition to the air arms of each. Its Interdictor Strike (pictured) and Air Defense Variants have fulfilled all expectations and are likely to remain in RAF service well into the next century.*

## Acknowledgments

**Austin Brown/The Aviation Picture Library,** pages 10, 11(top), 13, 18, 40, 42, 47, 48, 49, 50(below), 51, 53(top), 55, 63, 64, 67, 70, 71, 81, 90, 94(below), 103, 112, 122.
**Avions Marcel Dassault-Breguet Aviation,** pages 9, 11(below), 12(below), 17, 19.
**Bison Picture Library,** pages 34(below), 81, 112-3, 114.
**British Aerospace Aircraft Group,** pages 52, 60, 61, 62.
**Jeremy Flack/Aviation Photographs International,** pages 24, 25, 128.
**Michael J Gething,** pages 23, 31/US Department of Defense, pages 32, 33(both), 34(top).
**HQ RAF Germany/Barry Ellson,** page 65.
**M J Hooks,** pages 41, 50(top), 68-9, 75(top), 97/British Aerospace pages 59/McDonnell Douglas pages 77, 121.
**MARS/Klaus Niska,** pages 24(below), 27.

**McDonnell Douglas Corp-St Louis,** pages 76, 96, 107(below), 111, 115.
**Ministry of Defence,** pages 26, 35, 54, 95.
**Photri,** pages 74, 75(below).
**Saab-Scania,** pages 37, 38, 39, 43, 44-5.
**Salamander Books,** pages 28-9/Avions Marcel Dassault-Breguet Aviation, pages 20, 21.
**The Research House,** pages 82-4, 85, 88, 89, 101, 126/ANG pages 78-9/Dassault-Breguet, page 12(top)/E Nevil, page 53(below)/General Dynamics page 123/Grumman, pages 104-5, 106, 107(top)/Lockheed, page 68/MATRA, page 16/McDonnell Douglas, pages 117, 118-9, 120/RAF, pages 56-7/Mike Roberts, page 102/Thomson Brandt-Armements, pages 14-5/USAF, pages 72-3, 84, 98-9, 108, 110, 124, 125, 127/US Navy, pages 92-3.
**US Air Force,** page 109.
**Bill Yenne/American Graphic Systems,** pages 86, 87, 91, 94(top).

# CONTENTS

# INTRODUCTION

Protecting one's own territory from enemy attack must surely be the first rule of warfare no matter how it is waged. And ever since the first recorded use of aircraft to influence the course of ground action in the Turkish Empire in the early years of this century, this rule has applied in air warfare as anywhere else. Fighter aircraft are the sentries of the air – their mission to intercept and destroy those enemy aircraft intent on attacking their bases and lines of communication.

Speed, agility and firepower are the crucial attributes of any fighter – and the first two gained immeasurably from the advent of the turbojet during World War II. Britain's Gloster Meteor was fast enough to intercept even the notorious V1 'buzz bombs,' while Germany's equally impressive Messerschmitt Me262 was wasted by Hitler's insistence that it be used as an attack bomber, its speed negated by a heavy bomb-load when it could have been more usefully deployed against the marauding American 'heavies.' Nevertheless the turbojet gave the fighter a new lease of life and provided the world with new streamlined aircraft at which to marvel.

As with turbojet development, the West led the field – but the Soviets were not out of the race altogether: the Mikoyan-Gurevich design bureau quickly came to grips with the new technology and, basing their first fighter design round the British Nene turbojet, came up with the impressive MiG-15. But when the US F-86 Sabre bested the MiGs in the skies over Korea by a 9:1 kill ratio, it emphasized a technological gap that the Soviets were to take many years to close. Korea was significant, too, in that it was the first arena in which East and West fighter technology came face to face. Vietnam and the Middle East were to prove equally absorbing battlegrounds for the same reason, pitching Phantom against MiG-21 as the world looked on.

The third necessary attribute of a fighter, firepower, was to change no less significantly than everything else. In many ways the advances in engine and airframe technology had far outstripped the weaponry carried – the cannon of fighters of the 1950s could still be compared to the hand-held small-arms of World War I. By the 1970s developments in air-to-air missiles had revolutionized the face of air warfare to such an extent that dogfights could now be carried out from outside visual range. Infra-red and sophisticated radar-guided missiles provided a deadly choice of weapons for the modern duellists of the sky.

The biggest breakthrough since the turbojet itself came when the United States unveiled its supersonic 'Century Series' of fighters, so named after their three-figure designations. Though the first of these, the F-100 of the early 1950s, was a development of the Sabre, subsequent designs proved both innovative and striking in appearance. A noteworthy development at this time was reheat (afterburning), a technique of burning fuel in the engine exhaust to provide extra thrust for takeoff or combat, and such innovations were soon to see Mach 2 fighters enter frontline service.

In the 1970s, the Soviet Union finally emerged from the shadow of the United States to produce some impressive combat types that stood comparison with the best the West had to offer – a task eased in no small way by a comparative lack of the fiscal restrictions which hampered development in the West. Its most impressive fighter in performance terms, the Mach 3 MiG-25 Foxbat, was developed initially as a response to a cancelled project in the United States – but ironically the MiG-25, in turn, provided the catalyst for development of the F-15 Eagle.

France and Sweden proved that innovation in fighter design was not confined solely to the superpowers with aircraft of the quality of the Mirage, Draken and Viggen, while Britain made its mark by initiating development of the Panavia Tornado. This aircraft incorporated variable geometry, a concept which took some time to have any influence in the fighter field due to its complexity and a consequent weight penalty. Vertical takeoff remained a side issue for the same reason, although the British Aerospace Harrier, nominally a subsonic attack type, operated successfully as a ship-based fighter in the Falklands to prove that speed is not always the sole criterion in air combat.

As early as 1957, a British Government White Paper was prematurely writing off the fighter, predicting that manned aircraft would have no role to play in modern warfare. But time has proved the threat of airborne attack remains relevant in the nuclear age, despite the spotlight falling on Star Wars and its like. Paradoxically, as statesmanship reduces the risk of all-out nuclear war, so the emphasis falls once more on the manned bomber as a means of attack – and the fighter as its adversary. Faced with this scenario and the advent of 'stealth' technology, it seems unlikely that fighters will ever be written out of the armories of the major powers.

# FRANCE

Since World War II, the fiercely nationalistic French have given unquestioning support to their own aircraft industry, and have reaped deserved rewards – most notably in the jet fighter field. Unlike the majority of European countries, they have chosen to go it alone in fighter development, and will enter the next century with two fine examples of the breed in the Rafale and Mirage 2000.

The French fighter success story owes everything to Marcel Dassault, who rebuilt his country's aviation industry after the ravages of the German occupation in World War II. Active between the wars under his former name of Bloch, he went on to emulate the Soviet Union by using British aero-engine technology around which he based his first design, the Ouragan. When an indigenous jet engine, the SNECMA Atar, became available, his swept-wing derivative design, the Mystère, became the first European aircraft to exceed the speed of sound.

Dassault's name, however, will forever be linked with the Mirage, the generic name for a family of fighters, bombers and attack aircraft which first emerged in the mid-1950s and are set to continue as frontline *Armée de l'Air* types well into the next century. Design commonality giving minimal-cost development, led to variable geometry (the successful Mirage G) and VTOL (the unsuccessful III-V) sub-types.

France's decision to withdraw from NATO has reinforced their home-grown purchasing policy. But this independence has been offset by the lack of combat-testing opportunities available to the superpowers. That said, Israel has operated the Mirage successfully in combat and developed it into the IAI Kfir-C2. As if to provide further proof of the timelessness of Dassault's original design, the Mirage III's fixed-wing format was re-adopted for the Mirage 2000, the Mirage that will serve alongside the all-new Rafale in years to come.

Right: *Having decided not to participate in the European Fighter Aircraft program for a fighter of the 1990s, France embarked on a successor to the legendary Mirage in the Rafale. Unlike the EFA, the Rafale will double as a ground-attack type when it enters service in 1990, and is intended to replace the Jaguar in that role.*

Above: *First flown in 1949, the Dassault MD 450 Ouragan earned its place in the* Musée de l'Air *at Le Bourget, Paris, by being the first of a long and distinguished line of French-built jet fighters. The type's straight wing inevitably led to a subsonic performance, but even so it was used for several years as the mount of the Patrouille de France aerobatic team. Power for the Ouragan (Hurricane) derived from a license-built Rolls-Royce Nene engine developing 5004lbs (2270kg). It served into the 1960s with the Armée de l'Air and was exported to the air forces of Israel, India (as the Toofani) and, later, Salvador in the mid-1970s.*

Above right: *With 30 degrees of wing sweep, the Ouragan became the Mystère IIC. The type was the first French aircraft to break the sound barrier, albeit in a shallow dive. The Mystère IV introduced a longer fuselage and thinner wing, and could be identified by a narrow dorsal spine: after appearing in French colors in Suez in 1956 shortly after entering service, this variant saw much service with Israel as a fighter and ground-attack type in the many Arab-Israeli conflicts that followed.*

Right: *Marcel Dassault's name will forever be associated with the Mirage family of fighters, first flown in November 1956 and likely to feature strongly in the French fighter force well into the next century. The most numerous variant, the Mirage III, is marketed for export as the 5 and 50 with simplified electronics and is claimed to be the cheapest Mach 2 fighter available in the late 1980s. These Mirage 50s are pictured prior to delivery to Egypt.*

Left: *The Mirage 50 is rather more typical of the tailless delta-planform basic design which has now logged over 2.5 million flight hours in the service of 21 countries. The mix of underfuselage air-to-surface missiles and underwing drop tanks, with air-to-air missiles outboard, underlines the type's workhorse nature and versatility, having been marketed with great success as a fighter/ground-attack type to Middle East and Third World nations.*

Above left and above: *The experimental Dassault-Breguet Mirage III NG (Nouvelle Génération) retained the typical delta-wing planform of the mark but introduced small canard foreplanes for experimental handling purposes. These were first introduced in the Israel Aircraft Industries Kfir-C2, an unlicensed Mirage variant developed after a French arms embargo in the 1970s. In the absence of a conventional tailplane, these auxiliary flying surfaces are claimed to improve maneuverability in combat, as well as reducing take-off run and landing length.*

Overleaf: *The second prototype Mirage 2000 displays its firepower in the ground-attack role, unleashing a salvo of 68mm rockets. Five underfuselage and four underwing hardpoints with a potential ordnance load of 11,025lb (5000kg) give this Mirage sub-type, like its predecessors, an impressive multirole capability. The sixth Mirage variant, it first flew in March 1978 and, despite sharing the name, is in fact a completely different airframe.*

Above: *The Armée de l'Air employs the Mirage 2000 in several roles, one of which is interception. The pictured aircraft, resplendent in combat camouflage, carries a standard mix of radar-homing and infra-red-homing air-to-air missiles in the Matra Super 530 (inboard) and R.550 Magic (outboard) respectively, equippping it for any combat eventuality. The Super 530 was developed especially for the Mirage 2000, and, combined with the airframe/engine combination's impressive performance, makes it one of the world's outstanding interceptors.*

Above: *The two-seat Dassault-Breguet Mirage 2000N first flew in 1983. It is an all-weather strike derivative of the 2000B operational trainer design specially strengthened for prolonged low-level flight. The missile mounted under the fuselage is the ASMP (Air-Sol Moyenne Portée), launched by the navigator from his position in the rear cockpit, which possesses a nuclear capability. Even when deployed with a non-nuclear warhead, it can pinpoint tactical military targets such as bridges with impressive ease.*

Above: *The predatory shape of the Mirage 2000N prepares for touchdown. Its terrain-following radar assisted it in taking up the tactical nuclear strike role in 1988, in tandem with the previously mentioned ASMP, and the type may well end up supplementing the aging Mirage IVP in the strategic bomber role.*

Right: *A French Mirage 2000 shows off its altitude perfomance and rate of climb afforded by the new generation axial flow SNECMA M53 turbojet designed specially for high Mach flight and developing 19,840lbs (9000kg) thrust. With its state of the art digital weapons and radar systems, advanced titanium and boron/carbon fiber construction and electrical 'fly-by-wire' flight control system, the mark is clearly a fighter for the next century, sharing only the name and delta-wing planform of the earliest 1950s-vintage Mirages. Operational since 1984, the Mirage 2000 currently serves the air forces of six countries.*

Above: *Visible in this view of the Dassault-Breguet Rafale are the type's canard foreplanes, adopted to enhance maneuverability in combat and short-field performance. The wing also bears a distinctive double-delta kink similar – though not as exaggerated as – the Swedish Saab Draken. These and other innovations were adopted after lengthy tests, since the Rafale is destined to precede the French ACT (Tactical Combat Aircraft) and ACM (Naval Combat Aircraft) into service in the 1990s.*

Above: *First flown in July 1986, the prototype Rafale is intended as a technology demonstrator only, paving the way for deliveries to the French air force and navy in 1990. It is ultimately intended as a Jaguar replacement. As pictured, it carries a pair of Matra Magic air-to-air missiles on wingtip stations. Its underbelly weapons points can carry the Matra Mica missile.*

## USSR

In the postwar race to establish supremacy in jet fighter design, the superpowers of East and West started as equals – and as if to prove the point their first production jet fighter, the MiG-15, flew just three months after its counterpart in the United States, the similarly configured North American F-86. Combat in Korea proved the MiG's superior high-altitude performance was not enough to save it from decimation; first blood had been drawn by the United States.

In keeping with Soviet military and technological doctrine, steady refinement rather than innovation was the name of the game when Mikoyan updated the MiG-15 design to produce the MiG-17 and – when an indigenous axial-flow turbojet became available – unveiled the world's first supersonic production fighter in the MiG-19. Unfortunately, it could only exceed Mach 1 in a dive – and this qualification symbolized Soviet standing in the fighter development stakes.

The comparative freedom from the budgetary constraints faced by the West was a great advantage in clawing back some of the lost technological ground. Variable geometry was one field in which the Soviet Union was able to steal a march on its Western rivals, producing a capable combat fighter in the MiG-27 with considerably fewer teething troubles than the F-111. In speed, too, the Mach 3 MiG-25 Foxbat reigned supreme. And lest it be thought that Mikoyan-Gurevich remains the only design bureau to contribute to the Soviet order of battle, Pavel Sukhoi's Su-15 interceptor underlined its presence by bringing down flight KAL 007 in 1983 in an incident that had international repercussions.

Despite the distractions of the Afghanistan campaign, where danger stemmed from ground-launched missiles rather than airborne opposition, the Korean airliner incident showed the Soviet Union still places a premium on the defense of its airspace. The resuscitation of the B-1 project in the United States after its mid-1970s cancellation emphasized the continuing role of the manned bomber – and ensured a continuing place for the fighter in the Soviet armory for the forseeable future.

Right: *An unusual view of the Mikoyan-Gurevich MiG-23 with its variable-geometry wing in the fully swept position usually adopted for supersonic flight. Often likened to a smaller Phantom in terms of its capabilities, the Flogger (as it is codenamed by NATO) and its ground-attack derivative the MiG-27 is probably the most important Soviet tactical warplane currently in service.*

Left: *A line-up of preserved airframes from the Mikoyan-Gurevich design bureau showcases the MiG-17 in front of two MiG-21s and a MiG-23. Codenamed Fresco by NATO, the refined version of the early MiG-15 design saw action in Vietnam, where its maneuverability made it a better dogfighter than its predecessor had proved. Although it added an afterburner to the MiG-15's Klimov VK-1 turbojet, the MiG-17 still lacked supersonic perfomance in level flight.*

Above left: *The MiG-15 established the Mikoyan-Gurevich design bureau as leaders in Soviet jet technology – a position they retained into the 1980s. Aero-engine technology was initially borrowed from the West – power plant was a copy of the Rolls-Royce Nene by Klimov – and the result was a basic yet effective jet fighter with a maximum speed of Mach 0.92. Like Pakistan, in whose colors this MiG-15 trainer is pictured, many of the score of countries which operated the type went on to fly more sophisticated MiG products.*

Above: *Despite showing a marked family resemblance to its predecessors, the MiG-19 Farmer was a completely new twin-engined fighter design. After lengthy teething troubles, the re-engined MiG-19S replaced its Mikulin engines with 7165lb (3250kg) Tumansky RD-9 turbojets, this leading to a lengthy association between airframe and engine manufacturers. From 1958 the MiG-19 production line was situated not in the USSR but Czechoslovakia, where the line was moved to make way for the Mach 2 MiG-21. The pictured aircraft in Pakistan Air Force service is in fact an unlicensed copy of the MiG-19, one of some 1800 produced by the Shenyang works and known as the F-6 Fantan.*

Above: *Codenamed Fishbed by the NATO allies, the MiG-21 delta-wing single-seat interceptor stands as the most successful Soviet combat aircraft of all time and challenges the McDonnell Douglas F-4 Phantom for the title of most widely used jet fighter. Seen in Chinese air force service, the type's simplicity stemmed from Soviet pilots' experiences in Korea and reflected their wish for a maneuverable clear-weather interceptor. From 1961, when the MiG-21PF all-weather version became operational, the type was the subject of continuous improvement and remained in production over 25 years after its first flight as the experimentally designated E-5 in 1956.*

Above: *The earlier versions of the MiG-21, as exemplified by the pictured MiG-21F of the Finnish air force, were day interceptors with limited range and armament and were identifiable visually by the kinked, narrow vertical tail. Typically, two to four AA-2 Atoll or AA-8 Aphid air-to-air missiles would supplement the type's two 30mm cannon. Entering service in 1959, the MiG-21F was soon supplemented by more capable variants of the basic design. This view emphasizes the tailpipe of the 12,600lb (5750kg) thrust Tumansky turbojet.*

Overleaf: *Later models of the MiG-21 such as the pictured PFMA subvariant had a cockpit faired into the fuselage spine, a brake chute fairing at the base of the fin trailing edge, a wider vertical tail and sundry other refinements. A larger centerbody inside the engine inlet housed an improved radar. The pictured example, seen on an overseas exchange visit in the 1970s, carries underwing ferry tanks.*

27

Left: *A MiG-23 takes off on an operational sortie with its variable-geometry wing extended and all-swivelling horizontal tail surfaces clearly visible. On landing, the type deploys a brake parachute from a small bullet fairing on the trailing edge of the vertical tail. Fat tires and a mudguard on the nosewheel indicate a rough-field capability common among modern-day VG types.*

Above left: *An impressive line-up of MiG-23 Flogger variable-geometry fighters in East German service. The type first flew in 1966-7 and was the first swing-wing warplane to be developed in the USSR. Problems encountered with Flogger-A – notably in the tail and wing leading edge areas to improve stability – led to a second development period before the far more capable Flogger-B came on the scene in 1971-2. Its success led to export to all Warsaw Pact countries except Rumania, and led to it being hailed as the MiG-21's successor in the air-superiority role.*

Above: *A MiG-23S Flogger-B is pictured in France in 1978. Its dorsal fin, considerably smaller than that usually seen, suggests modifications to the type continued a decade after first flight in an attempt to improve maneuverability. The main landing gear, also seen to advantage in this view, is of complex design but is intended to save space, retracting as it does into the fuselage side. The type spawned its own specialist ground-attack derivatives, the MiG-27 Flogger-D and F, which differed in several important respects to the basic design.*

Above: *A Libyan example of the MiG-25 Foxbat lingers long enough to be photographed over the Mediterranean. With a maximum speed in level flight of Mach 3, the type can clearly leave pursuers in its wake. Although originally developed as an interceptor to counter the threat of the US B-70 supersonic bomber – the pictured Foxbat-A, operating in this role, carries the massive AA-6 Acrid air-to-air missiles – the type is now almost exclusively operated by the Soviet air force as a high-speed reconnaissance type. A defecting Soviet pilot flew a Foxbat-A to Japan in 1976, thereby providing the West with a fascinating insight into its design and equipment.*

Top: Clearly a development of the Foxbat airframe, the MiG-31 Foxhound was originally known to NATO as the Super MiG-25 or MiG-25M. Its additional crew member is accommodated in the distinctive large cockpit and operates the pulse-doppler radar for the four AA-9 missiles. These give the type a considerable edge over its predecessor, which it supplanted in the interceptor role in the mid-1980s. This weapons system can engage targets such as cruise missiles flying at heights as low as 150 feet, while its increased combat radius compensates for a decrease in maximum speed to Mach 2.4.

Above: The delta-wing Sukhoi Su-9 interceptor, seen here in its most numerous Fishpot-B variant, was designed to the same specification as the more widely used and better known MiG-21. Though never operated outside the Soviet Union, the Su-9 and its Su-11 development (Fishpot-C) provided the backbone of the Soviet air-defense force (PVO) until supplanted by the larger Su-15 in the late 1960s. Its closest Western counterpart was the English Electric (BAC) Lightning.

Left: *Although by no means as capable as its only comparable contemporary the British Aerospace Harrier, some 40 examples of the Yakovlev Yak-36 Forger are currently deployed operationally aboard the Soviet Navy's Kiev Class aircraft carriers. The type is supersonic at altitude, unlike the Harrier, but cannot vector in forward flight (VIFF) for added maneuverability since its lift engines are separate from its main cruise engine – and if one should fail to restart for landing the aircraft must be abandoned. Lacking a built-in gun armament and a search radar, the Yak-36 is necessarily limited in the air-to-air and air-to-ground roles but in the light of the subsonic Harrier's experience against the Mach 2 Mirage in the Falklands War the Forger has considerably more than nuisance value.*

Above left: *Sukhoi developed their Su-7 Fitter fighter-bomber into a semi-variable geometry type in which only the outer wing panels actually pivoted. The result was an aircraft whose load-carrying capability in its usual ground-attack role was increased but which retained the poor range characteristic of its fixed-wing forebear. Known as Su-17 in Soviet service, the type has been exported to Egypt, Peru, Poland and Libya: it is pictured in Libyan markings armed with a pair of AA-2 Atoll air-to-air missiles.*

Above: *Sukhoi's potent Su-15 Flagon all-weather interceptor is best known for its part in the destruction of the Korean Air Lines Boeing 747 that violated Soviet airspace in 1983. Unusually for an interceptor, it carries no gun or cannon armament, relying solely on a pair of AA-3-2 Advanced Anab missiles (one infra-red and one radar-homing). These are carried underwing; the pictured example is, of course, 'clean.' Despite the introduction of the MiG-31, the Mach 2 Su-15 is likely to remain a front-line Soviet interceptor for some while to come.*

# SWEDEN

In comparison with France, Sweden emerged from World War II with the distinct advantage of building an aircraft industry from a base of neutrality. They were quickly off the mark with the Saab-29, an unattractive but functional aircraft powered by a British Goblin engine that became Europe's first operational swept-wing fighter in 1951. Its name of 'Tunnan' (Barrel) was well deserved, but it served notice that Sweden had no intention of being left behind in the jet fighter development stakes.

The Lansen continued to build on imported aero-engine technology but did include a Swedish-developed afterburner. Its successor in 1955, the Draken, broke this predictable mold, its double-delta planform giving it one of the most distinctive shapes around. When the Mach 2 Draken was first mooted six years earlier, only the rocket-powered Bell X-1 had exceeded the speed of sound – an indication of the technological advances involved. Finland and Denmark were customers for the Draken, Sweden's first postwar aviation export.

Saab followed the Draken with something equally distinctive and, more importantly, tailored to Swedish needs. The Viggen's canard foreplanes were intended to assist short takeoff and permit dispersal to rough fields, roads or even icebound lakes in times of emergency. A Swedish-developed thrust reverser – the first in service on a supersonic turbojet or fan aircraft – shortened the Mach 2 fighter's landing roll quite dramatically.

The Viggen was a truly multi-role combat aircraft and its fighter, reconnaissance, attack and trainer variants will form the backbone of Sweden's air power by the end of the 1980s as part of the so-called System 37. From 1992, the similarly configured JAS39 Gripen will also be tasked with these roles, and doubtless carry on Saab's tradition of excellence. It is a tradition which enables Sweden to maintain its traditional neutral stance sandwiched as the country is between East and West.

Right: *From 1955 the Saab-32 Lansen (Lance) served the Swedish air force or Flygvapnet for nearly 25 years in a variety of roles. Similar in appearance to the British Hunter, to whose Rolls-Royce Avon engine its makers married a Swedish-developed afterburner, it was supersonic in a dive. Its exceptionally clean lines were marred only in the S32C by pods containing electronic countermeasures and reconnaissance sensors. This variant was the last to survive in service in the late 1970s.*

Above: *After converting the piston-engined J 21R to jet power as an interim measure, Sweden's Saab flew their first purpose-built jet in 1948. The J 29 was the first production fighter in Western Europe to feature a swept-back wing and, despite the portly appearance that gained it the name of Tunnan (barrel), it was comparable in performance with the American Sabre and Soviet MiG-15. The type served operationally from 1951 onwards in the fighter, attack and reconnaissance roles, putting Sweden firmly on the jet fighter map alongside the superpowers.*

Right: *A formation of four of the 600-plus J 29s ordered by the Swedish Flygvapnet; they served in a front-line role through the 1950s. Power was provided by a de Havilland Ghost turbojet, the power plant of the contemporary de Havilland Venom. Unlike the Venom, which adopted a twin-boom layout to permit the turbojet to exhaust freely, the J 29's engine vented under high-mounted tail surfaces, leading to a less than streamlined design. With its gaping engine intake, the J 29 remained determinedly subsonic.*

Above: *First flown in 1955, Saab's Draken
(Dragon) caused a stir with its double-delta wing
planform – but went on to equip the air forces of
Sweden, Finland and Norway: a two-seat
SK35XD of the latter nation is pictured. So
efficient was the design that it proved capable of
Mach 2 though originally designed to attain half
that speed – and this on a single Rolls-Royce
Avon engine, two of which powered the
considerably less streamlined British Lightning.
Armament of the fighter version consisted of four
Sidewinder AAMs and two Aden cannon. After
entering Swedish service in 1960, export orders
kept production lines rolling into the 1970s.*

Right: *Tail view of the Saab-37 Viggen
(Thunderbolt) showing the jet nozzle of the
26,015lb (11,800kg) thrust Volvo Flygmotor RM8A
afterburning turbofan. The unpainted metal
aperture is an integral thrust reverser, a Swedish
development and the first such to be fitted on a
supersonic afterburning turbojet or fan. It is an
important contributor to the Viggen's short
landing roll and hence its much-envied
combination of Mach 2 performance with the
ability to operate from short stretches of road or
grass away from easily-targeted airbases.*

Above: *An unusual view of the Viggen showing the canard foreplanes that became the type's trademark on its appearance in 1967. Saab followed one strikingly original design, the Draken, with another – and the Viggen proved even more successful than its predecessor. The pictured AJ37 is dedicated to the attack role with a secondary fighter capability: the interceptor fighter variant is designated JA37 and has a more powerful engine developing 28,150lbs (12,770kg).*

Above: *The Viggen in near-plan view, showing an impressive armament cache, including Sky Flash and Sidewinder air-to-air weapons. The center-line pylon can carry a drop tank (pictured) or multi-sensor reconnaissance pod, emphasizing the multi-role capability it shares with the Draken and the Lansen. The System 37 weapons system based around the Viggen may well never be emulated, such was the cost of development to a small and traditionally neutral nation such as Sweden.*

Overleaf: *Clearly emerging from the same design stable as its predecessor the Viggen, Saab's JAS 39 Gripen will enter service with Sweden in 1992. The canard foreplanes, so revolutionary in the Viggen's time, have now been adopted by the lightweight fighters of the next generation – the French Rafale, Israeli Lavi and the EFA (European Fighter Aircraft). Again like the Viggen, the lightweight Gripen – first flown in 1987 – has been designed to undertake fighter, attack and reconnaissance roles with minimum modification.*

# UNITED KINGDOM

The United Kingdom's early lead in jet fighter development can be traced directly to the work of engine pioneer Frank Whittle. But when German aero-engine secrets became common property after World War II, the lead did not last long. Early designs like the de Havilland Vampire harked back to wartime design and construction techniques; it took some time for airframe technology to catch up with engine development.

If British designs of the postwar decade were generally solid but unspectacular, the Hawker Hunter possessed several other virtues which guaranteed it a long service career. After serving the Royal Air Force with distinction, the (just) subsonic type went on to clock up over two decades as the backbone of several foreign air forces. The biggest success was the English Electric (later BAC) Lightning, a design based on a pair of RR Avon turbojets mounted one atop the other with a wafer-thin, raked-back plank of a wing and a pair of air-to-air missiles. This specialized Mach 2 interceptor was the only design to escape the damaging effects of the 1957 White Paper that dismissed the future value of manned fighters – a blow from which the industry took some while to recover.

Vertical takeoff was an area in which Britain *did* restore its early reputation for innovation. The result was the Harrier, ostensibly an attack aircraft whose fighter derivative, the Mach 2 P1154, was cancelled in 1966. The United States Marine Corps adopted the type as a combat aircraft, developing it into the AV-8 and pioneering VIFF (vectoring in forward flight) to give it almost infinite maneuverability. The Royal Navy's Sea Harrier had the chance to prove the type's mettle in the Falklands, emerging a world-beater.

More typical of modern fighter technology is the Mach 2 variable-geometry Panavia Tornado, developed in conjunction with Italy and West Germany in an attempt to overcome the massive development costs that bedevil most major projects in the 1980s. At the other end of the cost and complexity spectrum, the British Aerospace Hawk trainer has been adapted to carry air-to-air missiles and act as a last-ditch point defense interceptor. While neither type possesses the grace and elegance of a Spitfire, both could have important roles to play in the defense of their country alongside the EFA, the project intended to provide Britain, Germany, Spain and Italy with their main combat fighter in the next century.

Right: *The unmistakable British Aerospace Harrier, the first operational vertical take-off and landing fighter in the world. Nearly 30 years after its first flight as the P.1127 in 1960, the Harrier remains unrivalled by anything bar the far less capable Yak-36. Particularly noticeable in this view is the unusual main undercarriage configuration – tandem mainwheels (single at the nose, double aft).*

Above: *First flown in 1943, De Havilland's twin-boom Vampire combined the new turbojet propulsion with World War II-vintage construction, and was necessarily a stop-gap until airframe technology caught up with the aero engine's advance. Despite its obvious shortcomings, over 3000 examples were built and served with numerous air forces into the 1970s – notably with Switzerland, which retained over 30 examples late in that decade for pilot training alongside a developed Vampire variant, the Venom. A Royal Air Force T Mk II side-by-side two-seat trainer is pictured.*

Right: *Unlike its World War II contemporary the Messerschmitt Me 262, the Gloster Meteor had a very much unswept wing – and this gave the German jet a 120mph speed advantage. But combat between the types never took place, the Meteor's performance being more than a match for its only jet opponent in British skies, the unmanned V1 flying bomb. A preserved two-seat trainer example of the Gloster Meteor shows the type's straight-wing planform and twin Derwent engines in integral pods.*

Left: *After their retirement from Fleet Air Arm service in the 1970s, many Sea Vixens were modified for target towing duties, for which they swopped their familiar naval blue warpaint for high visibility red and yellow. This picture shows to effect the Sea Vixen's folding wing – essential for carrier operation – and hinged radar radome. Although retaining its military serial number and markings, this aircraft was operated by civilian contractors when the photograph was taken.*

Above left: *A pair of De Havilland Sea Vixen all-weather shipboard fighters practice 'buddy' air-to-air refuelling. The Sea Vixen duplicated the Vampire and Venom's configuration but its twin Rolls-Royce Avon turbojets conferred a far superior performance. Unusually, only the pilot of the two-man crew was visible in a bubble cockpit offset from the center-line, his companion being buried in the fuselage with his radar set. Along with the Hawker Siddeley Buccaneer, the Sea Vixen provided the backbone of Fleet Air Arm carrier-based air power in the 1960s.*

Above: *Designed by Sydney Camm, the man forever associated with the Hurricane, the Hawker Hunter flew in 1951 but was soon overtaken by genuinely supersonic types in the performance stakes: it could only exceed Mach 1 in a shallow dive. But its vice-free flying characteristics earned it a long career in Royal Air Force service as a fighter-trainer: the side-by-side two-seat training version of the Hawker Hunter designated T Mk 7 is pictured in the colors of RAF Training Command.*

Above: *A squadron of Hunters in full warpaint. The type found its true vocation as a ground-attack weapons platform, having natural stability and an enviable payload. The type's 10 underwing stores points and four Aden cannon enabled it to pack a fair punch with a variety of bombs and rocket packs. Although production of new Hunters ceased in 1966, a large number of the Royal Air Force's refurbished fighter and ground-attack variants eventually found their way into Middle Eastern ownership, a figure of over 700 being quoted.*

Above right: *A Hawker Siddeley Sea Hawk FGA Mk 6 carrier-borne strike fighter displays its folding wing on dry land at RNAS Culdrose. First flown in 1947, the type was principally manufactured by Armstrong Whitworth who produced all but the first 35. India, the Netherlands and West Germany joined the Fleet Air Arm as customers for a type whose straight-wing performance of Mach 0.79 quickly saw it relegated from front-line air combat duties and left it to concentrate on the attack role. Nevertheless, an airframe specially strengthened for shipboard duties proved exceptionally dependable and India continued to operate the type into the early 1980s.*

Right: *More often seen in camouflage or natural metal finish than the pictured gray drab, the BAC (formerly English Electric) Lightning was Britain's sole answer to the US Century Series of Mach 2 fighters. With the pilot mounted atop two Rolls-Royce Avon afterburning turbojets and a wafer-thin swept-back wing, the type had few attractive flying characteristics, yet its initial rate of climb was astounding at 50,000ft per minute. Entering RAF service in 1960, the Lightning remained a vital component of the British air defense system until replaced by the Panavia Tornado.*

Above: *Three Strike Command Lightnings, the nearest an F Mk 6 wearing the badge of No 5 Squadron, approach home base at Binbrook, Norfolk, in 1977. The type's ventral bay, clearly visible in this view, contains fuel and, frequently, a pair of 30mm Aden cannon to supplement the Red Top air-to-air missiles carried forward. The F Mk 6 was the ultimate RAF Lightning variant with nearly double its predecessors' fuel capacity and a cambered wing leading edge for operation at the greater weight this entailed. The smaller ventral bay of the leading aircraft, a two-seat trainer, can be compared with the two F Mk 6s with which it is pictured.*

Above: *Nose detail of the Harrier GR Mk 3, whose Ferranti Type 106 laser ranger and target seeker helps accurate delivery of air-to-ground weapons. Although the Harrier most often fulfills the close support and reconnaissance roles in Royal Air Force service, it can carry Aden cannon pods on center-line pylons for air-to-air combat. When out of range of friendly specialized interceptors (for example in the Falklands or Belize, where this aircraft was stationed) it is likely to find itself performing the interception role as well.*

Overleaf: *A Harrier launches an impressive salvo of rockets during training maneuvers. When flying operationally in the ground attack role, the Harrier will typically be operated as a STO/VL (Short Take-Off and Vertical Landing) type, raising its external ordnance to the maximum 8000lbs (3630kg) by making a conventional – though short – take-off run. Interestingly , the two-seat operational trainer has the same weapons-carrying capability as the single-seater, though its empty weight is higher.*

Above: *A Sea Harrier stands in the shadow of the 'ski-jump' training ramp at RNAS Yeovilton in Somerset. This duplicates the ramps fitted to the bows of Royal Navy* Invincible *Class cruisers on which the type is deployed and enables the Sea Harrier to take off with a greater weapons load than if forced to ascend vertically. Since the retirement of conventional aircraft carriers, the Harrier is the only fixed-wing shipboard type in the Fleet Air Arm inventory.*

Above: The Sea Harrier will always be associated with the vital role it played in the Falklands conflict in 1982. Equipped with air-to-air missiles like the pictured examples, they effectively protected the British fleet from air attack by Mirage fighters with over twice their maximum speed. A combination of new radar (the Ferranti Blue Vixen system) and AIM-20 advanced air-to-air missiles will give the Sea Harrier new teeth for the 1990s and beyond.

Above: *Despite its forbidding gray drab finish, this British Aerospace Hawk jet trainer is a most unlikely fighter. The Royal Air Force's standard intermediate flying and weapons trainer can carry two AIM-9L Sidewinder missiles, as in the pictured example, for airfield-defense duties in time of need. It is by no means the first jet trainer to fulfill such a dual role, having been preceded by the likes of the Aero L-39 Albatros (Czechoslovakia), the Macchi MB 339 (Italy) and the multi-nation Alpha Jet.*

Right: *Three examples of the British Aerospace Hawk formate for the camera. The nearest Hawk wears standard Training Command livery and lacks the wing hardpoints for underwing ordnance of the other two examples, which also feature a detachable 30mm Aden gun pod under the fuselage. This pod would normally be carried for weapons training along with rocket pods and up to six 1000lb (454kg) bombs underwing – all usually deployed against ground targets. An export market for heavier armed Hawks to double as light fighter-bombers has seen further experiments.*

Above: *The forbidding silhouette of the mighty
Panavia Tornado would normally spell destruction
to any enemy. With four Sky Flash missiles
tucked under the fuselage, a nose-mounted
27mm Mauser cannon and two Sidewinders
inboard of the wing-mounted drop tanks, this Air
Defense Variant (F Mk 3) Tornado normally
patrols the East German border and British home
airspace, where it has replaced the venerable
Lightning as principal interceptor.*

Right: *First flown in 1974, the Tornado was
developed by British Aerospace, Messerschmitt-
Bölkow-Blohm (Germany) and Aeritalia (Italy) for
their respective air forces. Two main sub-types
were planned: the IDS (Interdictor Strike) version,
known as the GR Mk 1 in Royal Air Force service,
and the Air Defense Variant (F Mk 3) with a 4ft
(1.2m) longer forward fuselage and pointed
radome containing a new radar known as
Foxhunter. A GR Mk 1 of No 9 Squadron Royal
Air Force is pictured.*

Left: *The Tornado's previous acronym, MRCA (Multi-Role Combat Aircraft), gives a clue as to the amazing diversity of stores it can carry. A true multi-mission aircraft, it can fulfill six different roles: close air support, interdiction, air superiority, interception, naval attack and reconnaissance. And despite a maximum offensive load-carrying capability of 18,000lb (8180kg) of stores, the Tornado is also optimized for operation from semi-prepared airfields thanks to its variable-geometry wing.*

Above: *Along with Panavia, the three-country consortium set up to develop the Tornado, a similar and complementary engine organization, Turbo Union, was entrusted with development of the type's two 15,000lb (6800kg) thrust RB.199 turbofans, seen here in afterburning mode. The variable-geometry wing is controlled by the pilot, and is seen here in the 66-degree fully-swept back position for high-speed flight: the angle of sweep can be reduced to 25 degrees to improve handling while landing.*

## USA

The change from the P (Pursuit) to F (Fighter) prefix for USAF fighters coincided with the advent of the P-80 Shooting Star, the equivalent of the British Meteor. The type's outmoded straight wing limited its potential, but with a multitude of companies – North American, Republic and Lockheed, for example – active in the field, the pace of development was rapid. And as the F-86 Sabre quickly proved in Korean skies, the results were potent indeed.

If the Sabre put the United States in front in the jet field, the 'Century Series' established something of an unassailable lead, as first Mach 1 and then Mach 2 was reached. But hand in hand with innovation came risk, and the Lockheed F-104 Starfighter earned the nickname of 'Widowmaker' in German service when losses rose to unacceptable levels in 1965. Low-level operations and poor maintenance were blamed, and the sophisticated but unforgiving 'flying missile' took time to overcome its reputation.

Crucial to fighter development in the United States was the dual roles played by the Air Force and Navy. A prime example of the cross-fertilization this created was the McDonnell Douglas F-4 Phantom, unquestionably the greatest United States' fighter of the postwar – or probably any – era. Originally intended as a shipboard interceptor, the Phantom proved an exceptionally versatile weapons platform, spawning a plethora of sub-variants in its 5000-plus production run and becoming one of the very few Navy types to be procured by the United States Air Force.

The 'fly-off' trials are another notable factor in fighter development; these require competing manufacturers to build prototypes for comparative evaluation. Thus the losing design to the General Dynamics F-16 in the USAF's LWF (Lightweight Fighter) competition took on a new lease of life when submitted to the US Navy as the F-18 Hornet.

The frontline fighter strength in the late 1980s shows a refreshing variety of shapes and sizes, from the lightweight F-16 Fighting Falcon to the Mach 2.5 F-15 Eagle, from the shipboard, swing-wing F-14 Tomcat to the twin-tail F-18. And if the bizarre, forward-swept wing of the Grumman X-29 is in any way indicative of the ATF (advanced tactical fighter) planned to take the United States into the next century, there may yet be stranger shapes to come.

Right: *The familiar shape of the McDonnell Douglas Phantom, the most successful Western jet fighter ever. Over 5000 examples of the bulky yet effective Mach 2 aircraft emerged from the production line after initial orders from the US Navy for 375 examples followed the type's first flight in 1958. Since then, over a dozen speed, time-to-height and altitude records have been rewritten by the F-4, which currently serves with the air arms of some ten countries. British examples like that pictured ordered for the Air Force and Fleet Air Arm utilized the home-grown Rolls-Royce Spey turbofans rather than the original General Electric J79 turbojets.*

Page 68-9, top: *Republic's F-84 Thunderjet was the last subsonic straight-wing jet fighter-bomber to serve with the US Air Force. Designed during wartime and first flown in February 1946, it was swiftly passed on to air forces of friendly nations under various aid programs as the successful Century Series of supersonic fighters took off. Though still subsonic, its swept-wing development, the F-84F Thunderstreak, proved a more potent performer.*

Page 68, below: *The Lockheed F-80 Shooting Star was the second American jet aircraft to fly after the experimental Bell P-59 Airacomet and saw much wider service. Powered by a de Havilland Goblin engine on first flight in January 1944, it was later re-engined with an indigenous power-plant when going on the serve the US Air Force as its first postwar jet fighter. The similar T-33 trainer derivative outlasted its fighter counterpart.*

Page 69, below: *First flown in 1947, the legendary North American F-86 Sabre ensured its place in aviation history by gaining mastery of the skies over Korea in the world's first jet-versus-jet combats against the MiG-15. In April 1948 it had become the first US fighter to exceed the speed of sound, and though subsequently surpassed by the Century Series (including its Super Sabre derivative), it soldiered on into the 1980s with the air forces of several Third World countries.*

Above left: *Despite its own excellent indigenous fighter designs, France called upon the North American F-100 Super Sabre to bolster its defenses in the 1950s. The 'Hun,' as it was affectionately known to USAF pilots, was first of the Century Series of supersonic fighters and was the first to exceed Mach 1 in level flight. A series of accidents blighted the type's early career, but well over 2000 had been produced by the time production ended in 1959 – a creditable achievement for what had started out as a private-venture development of the earlier Sabre with 45 degrees of wing sweep.*

Above: *Unusual in possessing no flaps – ailerons were fitted where flaps would normally have been – the F-100 Super Sabre has seen service in many unlikely forms. Along with the F-105 Thunderchief, the two-seat F-100F combat trainer was pressed into service with no little success in Vietnam against surface-to-air missile sites in Wild Weasel operations, while the pictured example has been modified as a drone under the designation QF-100 and operated by civilian contractors Flight Systems Inc.*

Overleaf: *A McDonnell F-101 Voodoo of the Maine National Guard fires one of its three AIM-4D Falcon air-to-air missiles from the retractable weapons bay in its underbelly. Originally ordered by USAF Strategic Air Command as a long-range bomber escort, the type survived cancellation on the grounds of insufficient range to play a vital role in the US air defenses. Many Air National Guard Voodoos were subsequently modified as RF-101s, with nose-mounted cameras.*

Above: *A preserved example of the F-101B, the two-seat version of McDonnell's Voodoo interceptor. Some 480 examples of this variant saw service with the US Air Defense Command, and 66 were later sold to the Canadian Armed Forces, with which they were designated CF-101B.*

Above right: *Pictured at Wethersfield Air Force Base, England, in 1960, this is an example of the F-101A, the first production Voodoo to enter service. Two of its four nose-mounted M-39 20mm cannon can be seen in this view, while three Falcon air-to-air missiles in an internal bay completed the type's armament. Subsequent marks dropped the cannon and added two Genie missiles on underwing hardpoints.*

Right: *The F-101B remained a vital link in the NORAD (North American Air Defense Command) chain for many years, setting new records for safety and low maintenance burden among USAF fighters as it did so. Apart from serving the US and Canada, a number of export examples of the supersonic fighter were also operated by Taiwan.*

Above: *The Voodoo continued in service into the late 1970s with US Air National Guard units, displaying impressive longevity for a type that was originally cancelled prior to its first flight in 1954. Relatively few Voodoos wore camouflage paint, the majority sharing the bare metal finish of the early example pictured.*

Above: *The F-101A Voodoo had originally been developed as an escort fighter for manned bombers like the B-36, but lack of range precluded this. Despite such problems, the mark created a world absolute speed record of 1208mph (1944km/h) and could attain Mach 1.5 at altitude.*

Above: *Known to its pilots as the 'Deuce,' the F-102 Delta Dart interceptor ran into teething problems aplenty with speed and ceiling both disappointing. After area-ruling the fuselage like a Coke bottle, the designers beat the problem and finally reached Mach 1. The picture shows two Air National Guard Delta Darts taking off.*

Above: *Even with auxiliary fuel tanks underwing, the clean unfettered lines of the Convair F-106 remain admirable. Yet since its introduction to US Aerospace Defense Command in 1959 the type was the subject of a continual updating program which continued until its eventual withdrawal in the early 1980s. Improved radar, a flight refuelling capability and drop tanks suitable for supersonic flight were among the modifications that kept the F-106 in the front line.*

Overleaf: *A Convair F-106 Delta Dagger of the California Air National Guard unleashes a Douglas AIR-2 Genie rocket. This was normally supplemented in the type's internal weapons bay by a clutch of four AIM-4 Super Falcons, while some were also fitted with a single 20mm cannon.*

Right: *A predatory-looking F-106A undergoes maintenance prior to operations. Although similar in appearance to the F-102 and originally designated F-102B, the F-106 was a considerably more capable aircraft with a maximum speed of Mach 2.3 as opposed to the Mach 1.25 of its troubled predecessor.*

Above: A Delta Dagger awaits flight. Despite delays in the development program due to Delta Dart hold-ups diverting funds, which resulted in only 35 percent of proposed deliveries, the type served for over two decades in the air defense front line before being replaced by the McDonnell Douglas F-15 Eagle.

Right: One of the many improvements applied to the F-106 during its years of service from 1959 was an ejector seat that could be operated in supersonic flight. A two-seat combat training version of the Delta Dagger, designated F-106B, saw limited service alongside its single seat contemporary. Some 63 examples of this combat-capable version were delivered.

Above: *A Lockheed F-104G Starfighter of the Luftwaffe's Luftversuchsregiment 1 stands alone on the airfield. Lack of hangar protection for this sophisticated warplane was just one of the theories behind a severe attrition rate sustained during the mid-1960s when one German Starfighter was being lost every ten days – a flashback to events after the US-built type's first flight in 1954 when four years of difficulties blighted its progress to operational status. Ultimately, improvements in maintenance practices and more familiar pilots reduced this to acceptable proportions, although the wisdom of tasking a specialized Mach 2 interceptor with low-level missions was questionable.*

Above: *Unperturbed by Germany's experiences, the Netherlands ordered the F-104G in quantity, encouraged by their participation in a European consortium to build it. Known as the Super Starfighter, this was, on paper at least, the most advanced fighter in the world when first mooted in 1959. The seven-year program helped rebuild the European aerospace industry and provide Germany, Belgium, Norway, the Netherlands, Italy, Turkey, Denmark and Spain with a semi-indigenous Mach 2 fighter.*

Above: *The Lockheed Starfighter's futuristic 'manned missile' shape originally derived from US pilots' combat experiences in Korea. Speed and altitude were paramount considerations in the two years of research that preceded its first flight in 1954. Over 25 years later, the German Navy were still using the F-104G Starfighter as front-line defense in the crucial Baltic region, though it was soon to give way to the Tornado.*

Above: *Last of the six Century Series fighters to fly when first flown in 1955, the all-weather Republic F-105 Thunderchief was designed to replace the F-84 Thunderjet in USAF service. In Vietnam, the single seat F-105D (the main production variant) and F-105F two seater proved especially effective in the strike role, with 14,000lbs (6350kg) of stores carried externally and in an internal bomb-bay. The F-105F also operated as a Wild Weasel type, hitting SAM missile sites in Vietnam with Shrike anti-radiation missiles. Its rugged construction meant most F-105s lived to fight another day.*

Overleaf: *A formation of five Republic F-105 Thunderchiefs from the US Air Force's 35th Tactical Fighter Wing pictured in 1980, at which time they were about to be relegated to Air National Guard duties. Known as the Thud or Lead Sled, the F-105 paid lip service to its 'F-for-fighter' designation with a 20mm Vulcan cannon – one of the most powerful aircraft guns in the world – but was first and foremost a strike aircraft in reality.*

Left: *A Phantom taxies out for take-off. Its two General Electric J79 turbojets give the F-4 a maximum rate of climb in clean configuration approaching 50,000ft/min (15,300m/min), fitting it perfectly for the role of inteceptor. When operating as a reconnaissance and photography platform, like the pictured RF-4C, speed and altitude are important considerations: the Phantom has set world records in both. It recorded a speed of Mach 2.6 (1606.3mph, 2585km/h) in 1961, having attained a record altitude of 98,537ft (30,034m) three years earlier.*

Above left: *The enormous 'saw-tooth' air intakes of the F-105 Thunderchief cast a shadow on its fuselage. In its quarter-century of service, the type established a reputation for all-round mission capability that would be hard to equal – and proved it under combat conditions in Vietnam. Its single 26,500lb (12,020kg) Pratt & Whitney J75 engine was thirsty for fuel – hence the ubiquitous drop-tanks – but gave it a Mach 2 speed in clean configuration.*

Above: *A Royal Air Force Phantom of Strike Command's No 29 Squadron banks to port, exposing an impressive selection of weaponry. Royal Air Force Phantoms on interception duties will typically carry a mix of infra-red Sidewinder and radar-guided Sparrow air-to-air missiles, as seen here.*

Left: *It should never be forgotten that the ubiquitous Phantom started life modestly in 1953 as the private venture F3H-G shipboard fighter. By the 1980s, the US Navy and Marine Corps, its intended customers, had taken delivery of almost exactly a quarter – 1264 – of the 5000-plus examples produced. The pictured Phantoms are F-4Bs, the first major production variant optimized for shipboard operation.*

Above: *Sixty years after Alcock and Whitten Brown's historic Atlantic crossing in a Vickers Vimy in 1919, this Royal Air Force Phantom made the journey in a fraction of the time – one of the smaller milestones the F-4 contributed to aviation history. Note the air inlets for the British variant's Rolls-Royce Spey engines, which are considerably wider than those of the standard J79-powered Phantom.*

Overleaf: *A US Air Force F-4E deploys its drag 'chute on landing. The USAF broke their tradition of not ordering Navy designs with an initial order for 583 Phantoms in 1963, singling out the F-4 as an exceptional aircraft indeed: the F-4E was the most numerous production variant. In keeping with its shipboard origins, land-based Phantoms invariably retain the arrestor hook under the tail, and when suitable wires are deployed this can reduce landing roll still further.*

Above: *An RF-4C photo-reconnaissance Phantom's distinctive extended nose profile betrays the presence of the camera inside. Most Phantom marks could be ordered in this form, and also carried extensive electronic countermeasures equipment. The nose-mounted Vulcan cannon is deleted to make way, but other weapons-carrying functions remain unchanged.*

Right: *All marks of Phantom are capable of receiving air-to-air refueling to extend a maximum ferry range of 1610 miles (2593km) still further. While early examples had to employ a front fuselage probe, the F-4C and subsequent variants featured a much neater dorsal 'pop-up' receptacle, partly obscured in this view.*

Above: *When it entered service in 1972, the Grumman F-14 Tomcat was entrusted with the long-range fleet-defense duties originally intended for the cancelled naval version of the General Dynamics F-111, the F-111B. Like the aircraft it replaced, the F-14 employed a variable-geometry wing but in all other respects was more technologically advanced. Since 1972 problems with engine reliability have necessitated an improvement program for the type's Pratt & Whitney TF30 turbofan power plants. The pictured aircraft prepares for an assisted take-off from the USS* John F Kennedy.

Right: *The distinctive front-on view of the Tomcat shows the unusual width between the engine inlet ducts each side of the cockpit: these are separated by large integral fuel tanks. The flat area above this extra-wide fuselage provides much additional lift, permitting extraordinary angles of attack of up to 60 degrees. Also of note are the twin vertical tail surfaces, canted outwards – the F-14 was one of the first aircraft to boast this now-popular tail configuration.*

Overleaf: *An F-14 waits its turn in the catapult aboard the carrier USS Nimitz. The radar contained in its nose is the Hughes AWG-9, specially developed for the AIM-54A Phoenix missiles it carries but originally intended for the still-born General Dynamics F-111B. It can identify individual targets in flight over 100 miles away before individually targeting up to six missiles to hit them.*

Above: *A Tomcat of US Navy squadron VF-42, based at Oceana, Va, shows off a full load of six Phoenix air-to-air missiles. Although costly, the Phoenix's 125-mile (200km) range makes it the longest-range AAM in service. A carrier air wing will usually include two F-14-equipped squadrons, while the type also serves with the US Marine Corps.*

Above right: *An F-14 from VF-145, flying from the USS* Dwight D Eisenhower, *adopts the fully-forward wing sweep angle of 20 degrees to formate with the photographing aircraft. As the wing pivots backwards to a maximum sweep angle of 68 degrees, retractable foreplanes or glove vanes emerge from the wing root at the leading edge to prevent pitching and to control alterations in the center of pressure. An automatic flight-control system takes care of wing sweep during combat.*

Right: *The prototype long-range interdiction and night fighter F-15 for the US Air Force, designated F-15E. The Martin Marietta LANTIRN (Low Altitude Navigation and Targeting InfraRed for Night) system carried on external pylons enables this variant of the Eagle to reproduce the type's impressive daytime combat capability in darkness. Conformal fuel tanks outboard of the engines extend range.*

Above: *With four Sidewinder and four Sparrow air-to-air missiles, more electronics than any combat aircraft previously built to target them and a Mach 2.5 performance to help deliver them, the McDonnell Douglas F-15 Eagle can justifiably claim the title of the West's premier fighter – at least until the next century. Developed as a 'Foxbat killer' to combat the Soviet MiG-25 with its Mach 3 performance, the F-15 emerged from the same stable as the Phantom in 1972.*

Right: *Four Eagles of the 49th Tactical Fighter Wing based at Holloman, New Mexico. The type's clean lines derive from the fact that every last item of the extensive early warning and countermeasures equipment it carries on board was intended for inclusion at the design stage. As a result, however, all weapons, except the nose-mounted 20mm M61 cannon, are carried externally.*

Above: *Compared with many modern jet fighters, the F-15's cockpit is relatively uncluttered. The type's sophisticated head-up display, a cathode ray tube, relays to the pilot all relevant information on his target from the Hughes APG-63 pulse-doppler radar and the weapons he needs to carry out an attack. The 'flying surfaces' visible in this unusual air-to-air close-up are in fact the top of the enormous engine air intakes.*

Right: *An F-15 shows off the 40,000ft/min (12,200m/min) rate of climb afforded by its two afterburning Pratt & Whitney F100 engines, each developing 23,800lbs (10,980kg) thrust. The F-15 eclipsed its Soviet rival the Foxbat in most performance areas barring sheer speed, attaining 'only' Mach 2.5. Its astounding thrust to weight ratio, far greater than any previous jet fighter, not only gave a good rate of climb but a service ceiling of 63,000ft (19,200m).*

Left: *A prototype F-16 turns on the reheat which, together with its simplicity and resulting minimum weight, gives it an impressive Mach 1.8 maximum speed. The type was developed in response to a US Air Force design competition in 1974 for a lightweight fighter: deliveries began four years later to the USAF and the air forces of Belgium, the Netherlands, Denmark and Norway.*

Above: *Three USAF General Dynamics F-16 fighters with underwing ferry tanks and wingtip-mounted Sidewinder missiles. Built around just one of the Pratt & Whitney F100 turbofans that powered the mighty F-15, the F-16 Fighting Falcon was intended as a maneuverable, lightweight single-seater to replace the F-104 Starfighter in the air forces of the United States and several European countries – and, as with the F-104, European production followed.*

Above: The wing surface of the F-16 varies in camber as airspeed increases. While cruising at subsonic speeds the wing is flat, while it curves lightly upwards once supersonic. The leading edge droops for subsonic maneuvers to increase lift from what is a very small wing by any standards. The trailing edge surfaces, known as flaperons, give the F-16 an enviable rate of roll.

Right: Originally developed by Northrop as the YF-17 to compete in the USAF LWF competition, the McDonnell Douglas F-18 enjoyed a new lease of life with the US Navy. Bearing the same relationship to the F-14 as the USAF's F-16 to the heavier F-15, it found a niche as a low-cost, multi-mission fighter. A new radar, increased fuel tankage and structural strengthening for catapult launch produced a capable new type which was ordered in quantity by the US Navy and Marine Corps.

Page 116, top: Front view of the F-18 reveals a similarity to the F-16 (with which it competed, unsuccessfully, to become the US Air Force Lightweight Fighter) and the F-14, whose canted vertical tail surfaces it borrowed. Two General Electric F404 engines, each developing 16,000lbs (7257kg) thrust give the type a maximum speed of Mach 1.8.

Page 116, bottom: An F-18 demonstrator prepares for take-off at the Paris Air Show, Le Bourget, in 1981. When the type first flew in 1978, the US Navy and Marine Corps announced their intention to purchase over 1350 Hornets of varying kinds, while export potential was envisaged for both the shipboard fighter and a land-based variant designated F-18L. Northrop, the company which originated the design, were responsible for the marketing of this subtype.

Page 117: The F/A-18 variant of the Hornet was intended for operation by the US Marine Corps. It retains the wingtip-mounted Sidewinder air-to-air missile armament, but otherwise has instruments and sensors configured for the ground-attack role. In addition, the service earmarked 30 examples of the two-seat variant for tactical air control.

Previous pages: *The agility and responsiveness of the F/A-18 has led to the type being selected as the mount of the US Navy's Blue Angels aerobatic team. Identical in every respect to their carrier-borne counterparts, the team's six Hornets are pictured in formation.*

Above: *Features like the folding wing shown here were obligatory modifications to the Hornet's original design to produce a carrier-borne fighter that can easily be stowed in below-deck hangars where space is necessarily limited. This F-18 awaits transport below.*

Right: *The F-18 undergoes ship-borne trials before attaining operational status in the early 1980s. In taking over Northrop's development of the type, McDonnell Douglas could call upon the experience of building thousands of aircraft for the US Navy, including the F-4 Phantom, A-3 Skywarrior and A-4 Skyhawk. Northrop remained responsible for 40 percent of the construction work on Navy F-18s.*

Above: *Apparent in this view of this General Dynamics F-111E is the nose radome for the General Electric APQ-123 multirole radar, two-seat side-by-side cockpit arrangement – somewhat unusual for a jet combat aircraft – and the rotating 'gloves' protruding above the wing at the leading edge hinge points.*

Right: *The effectiveness of the F-111's camouflage is apparent in this plan view, which also serves to show the variable-geometry wing in a cruise position midway between fully swept and unswept. Now a tried and tested formula for warplanes of East and West alike, the variable geometry concept pioneered by the F-111, the world's first production 'swing-wing' warplane, was not achieved without losses and modifications – and even groundings when three aircraft were mysteriously lost in Vietnam in 1968.*

Above: *Bombing-up an F-111 before a sortie. Like the Thunderchief it replaced in USAF service, the F-111 belied its fighter designation by being operated almost exclusively as an all-weather attack aircraft: an old-fashioned fighter-bomber with the emphasis on the latter role. Many are based in Britain, and it was aircraft from there that carried out the notorious raid on Libya in April 1986.*

Above: *A General Dynamics F-111 is pictured with its wing in the swept-forward (16 degree) position, giving the most economical fuel consumption for maximum 'loiter' capability. A range of over 3150 miles (5090km) is claimed with the aid of external fuel tanks. The disappointments of the F-111's checkered career – deficiencies in weight and performance of airframe and avionics – should not be allowed to overshadow its achievement in bringing variable geometry technology from the drawing board to the front line.*

Overleaf: *The predatory shape of the Saab Viggen, Sweden's premier front-line fighter until the advent of the Gripen in the 1990s. The two types share the characteristic shoulder-mounted canard foreplanes visible here. Like many modern fighters, the Viggen carries no fixed gun armament, a range of air-to-air missiles or gun pods providing its teeth.*